W9-DFZ-215

Margaret —

TOUCHING
*H*EARTS,
TEACHING
GREATNESS

Best Wishes!!

Touching *Hearts*, Teaching Greatness

STORIES FROM A COACH THAT TOUCH
YOUR HEART AND INSPIRE YOUR SOUL

TOM KRAUSE

**Andrews McMeel
Publishing**

Kansas City

01 02 03 04 05 KWF 10 9 8 7 6 5 4 3 2 1

Library of Congress Cataloging-in-Publication Data
Krause, Tom, 1957-
    Touching hearts, teaching greatness : stories from a coach that touch your heart and inspire your soul / Tom Krause.
        p. cm.
    ISBN 0-7407-1914-9
    1. Conduct of life. I. Title.

BJ1597 .K73 2001
170'.44—dc21   2001028972

DEDICATED TO
ALL MY STUDENTS,
PAST, PRESENT,
AND FUTURE

CONTENTS

INTRODUCTION

FOR OVER TWENTY YEARS I have been privileged to teach and coach thousands of wonderful students. This book is a collection of my favorite stories and poems inspired by them. The stories come from treasured memories. The poems come from the heart.

My wish is that this book serve as an inspiration to you. I hope what you read here will touch you forever. Remember, when you touch a heart, you change the world.

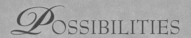OSSIBILITIES

When your dreams start to seem so impossible,
when roadblocks are all you can see,
look beyond all the problems that face you
and focus on possibilities.

Don't limit your thoughts to the present
or solutions you have learned from the past.
Remember to keep looking forward—
you may find the answer at last.

It is you who determines your future:
how your journey through tomorrow will be.
To fill all your days with adventure,
dare to see what no one else dares to see.

So never let obstacles stop you
or keep you from doing your part.
Have faith that your dreams are all possible
if you truly believe in your heart.

1

_B_ELIEVING
IN
_Y_OURSELF

COURAGE IS TRYING
WHEN YOU KNOW
YOU CAN LOSE.

MARK'S CHOICE

"WHAT'S WRONG?" I remember asking my team-
mate that question as he sat in front of his locker
more than twenty years ago. It was our senior
year in high school. We had just finished polish-
ing off another opponent, but there he sat: head
in hands, alone, in pain. He was tough, seventeen years old and a great athlete. His name was
Mark Overstreet.

The rest of our teammates had showered and left for home, but Mark was still fully dressed in his football uniform. When he raised his head to speak, I saw tears in his eyes. Now I knew something was really wrong. This was a young man who was more likely to make his opponents cry on the football field. "I don't know," he said softly. "It's as if all the injuries I've ever had are coming back. My whole body hurts. My legs feel like they weigh a hundred pounds each."

A week or so earlier, an outbreak of swine flu had swept through our community. One by one, everyone had lined up to take the vaccine to prevent the spread of the illness. All the students had the shot and thought nothing of it. When Mark received the vaccine, however, his body developed a very rare allergic reaction—so rare that his sudden illness was not correctly diagnosed until ten years later.

The morning after our conversation in the locker room, Mark woke to find his right foot "asleep." No matter how much he tried to rub the foot to alleviate the pins-and-needles feeling, the circulation never returned. Concerned, Mark's mother took him to the doctor. Mark's life was about to change forever.

Baffled by what he saw in his examination, the doctor was somber. "I don't know what's wrong with you, Mark, but you are going to lose that foot."

"No!" his mother exclaimed, in shock.

Stunned, Mark said, "What are you talking about? What's wrong with me?" The doctor couldn't answer that question. He admitted Mark to the hospital for further tests.

While he was in the hospital, Mark's left foot fell asleep and, just like the right one, never woke up. Not only were both feet losing circulation, but things were getting worse. After many failed tests the doctor entered his room to tell him the news. "Mark, whatever it is, it's killing you. It's spreading to your heart. We have only one hope. To try to stop the spread, we want to amputate both legs just below the knee. If that doesn't work, you have two weeks."

Two weeks? Two weeks for a young man who had never been sick a day in his life? "What's wrong with me?" Mark asked again.

"We don't know," the doctor said. Mark had to prepare for the operation without knowing his chances.

When the amputation was over, Mark woke to find the doctor by his bed. "I've got some good news and some bad news," the doctor said. "The good news is, you are going to live. Whatever it was, it's gone. The operation was success-ful. The bad news is, you are probably going to be in a wheelchair your whole life, and in and out of the hospital."

At this moment Mark made his decision, a choice that would shape his whole future. "No," he said. "I'm not staying in the hospital and I'm not staying in a wheelchair. I'm going to walk and I'm going to live my life! This is just the beginning, not the end."

It took a year, but after learning to use his artificial legs, Mark walked out of the hospital for the last time. Later, he decided that if he couldn't play football or baseball again, he would become a coach and teach others to play.

While in college, Mark met Sharon and fell in love. Sharon didn't mind Mark's prosthetic legs. She loved him for who he was—not who he wasn't. After graduation they married, and Mark began teaching handicapped students and coaching high school football. He and Sharon had four beautiful children. Mark is a high school principal in southwest Missouri—and my boss. Every morning Mark gets up, puts on his legs, and goes to school to greet students and teachers alike. If he ever has a bad day, you would never know.

Mark had a choice. He could be in that wheelchair, in and out of the hospital, feeling sorry about the bad break he suffered in high school. Some people choose to let bad breaks ruin their lives. But not Mark. He took a different path. He chose to live his life. He is an inspiration. ■

Some people sit, some people try.
Some people laugh, some people cry.

Some people will, some people won't.
Some people do, some people don't.

Some people believe and develop a plan.
Some people doubt—never think that they can.

Some people face hurdles and give them their best.
Some people back down when faced with a test.

Some people complain of their miserable lot.
Some people are thankful for all that they've got.

And when it's all over—when it comes to the end—
some people lose out and some people win.

We all have a choice. We all have a say.
We are spectators of life, or we get in and play.

Whichever we choose—how we handle life's game—
The choices are ours. No one else is to blame.

Tina's Ten Points

SHE WAS SEVENTEEN years old and always wore
a bright smile. This may not seem unusual—
but Tina Larson was born with cerebral palsy,
a condition that left her muscles stiff and
unmanageable. Because she had trouble speaking, this bright smile was the true reflection of
her personality.

Tina was a great kid. She used a walker

most of the time to navigate through the crowded hall-ways at school. A lot of people didn't speak to her. Why? Who knows. Maybe because she looked different, and the other students didn't know how to approach her. Tina usually broke the ice with people she met in the halls, especially the boys, with a big "Hi!"

The assignment was to memorize three stanzas of the poem "Don't Quit." I made the assignment worth only ten points, because I figured most of my students wouldn't do it. When I was in school and a teacher assigned a ten-point homework assignment, I sometimes blew it off. I was expecting about the same from my students. Tina was in the class, and I saw her normal bright smile change to a look of worry. Don't worry, Tina, I thought to myself, it's only ten points.

The day the assignment came due, I went through my roster, and my expectations were met as one by one each student failed to recite the poem. "Sorry, Mr. Krause," was the standard reply. "It's only worth ten points anyway, right?" Finally, in frustration and half kidding, I proclaimed that the next person who didn't recite the poem perfectly had to drop to the floor and give me ten push-ups. (This idea was left over from my days as a physical education teacher.) To my surprise, the next student was Tina.

Using her walker, Tina moved to the front of the class and, straining to form the words, began to recite the poem. She made it to the end of the first stanza—and made a mistake. Before I could say a word, she threw her walker to the side, dropped to the floor, and started doing push-ups. I was horrified. I wanted to say, Tina, I was just kidding! But she pulled herself back up in her walker, stood in front of the class, and began again. This time she finished all three stanzas perfectly, one of only a handful of students who did.

When she finished, a fellow student said, "Tina, why did you do that? It's only worth ten points!"

Tina took her time forming the words, "Because I want to be like you guys—normal."

Silence fell on the whole room, until another student exclaimed, "Tina, we're not normal—we're teenagers! We get in trouble all the time!"

"I know," Tina said, and a big smile spread across her face.

Tina got her ten points that day. She also got the love and respect of her classmates, and to her that was worth a lot more. ■

TOUCHING HEARTS

*D*ARE TO *B*ELIEVE

If you dare to believe,
to follow your star . . .

If you seek out your purpose
to learn who you are . . .

If you call on your courage,
find hope in your heart . . .

If you challenge your talent
to fulfill its part . . .

If love for your neighbor
helps shape who you are . . .

If you still can have faith
when you've traveled so far . . .

If troubles and setbacks
can't stand in your way . . .

If you find the resolve
to live life every day . . .

Then what you will find
at the end of the road

is strength in your heart
and peace in your soul.

2

$\mathscr{K}$EEPING PERSPECTIVE

TALENT WITHOUT
HUMILITY IS WASTED.

HOW A PERSON WINS AND LOSES
IS MORE IMPORTANT THAN HOW
MUCH A PERSON WINS AND LOSES.

37x—THE COACH'S LESSON

IT WAS THE FOOTBALL coach's favorite play: 37x. It was the play he ran first every game, a simple handoff to the fullback over left tackle. It was nothing special—just basic football.

When the young junior varsity football team took the field that night, the sophomore linemen knew what the first play would be: 37x. As they broke the huddle, however, they were greeted with a sight that spelled certain failure for the coach's favorite play. There, lined up over left tackle, was the biggest junior varsity defensive player they had ever seen. He was huge, nearly 300 pounds, and mean-looking. As the play unfolded, the fullback ran right into the mammoth defensive lineman and fell to the ground. It was like running into a brick wall. As the fullback picked himself up and staggered back to the huddle, he yelled at his linemen to block. "Block?" replied the linemen. "We can't block this guy. He's too big! Tell Coach to run another play."

The wide receiver came from the side of the field. He ran up to the quarterback and said, "Coach said run Thirty-seven X again." Unwillingly, the linemen broke the huddle and prepared to run the hopeless play. The results were the same: *crunch*—pain—no gain. The huge player taunted the offense to keep running that play. When the coach sent in the next play and it was again 37x, the huddle was outraged. Snap—handoff—*boom*. Same results: *crunch*—pain—no gain. "Punt!" yelled the coach from the side of the field.

After the punt the quarterback ran over to try to explain the situation. "Coach," said the quarterback, "we're not going to be able to run Thirty-seven X tonight. They have this big defensive lineman lined up right in the way. Our linemen can't block him. I think they're scared."

"I'll take care of it," the coach said. The second possession followed the same scenario as the first. The coach called 37x three more times, with the same disastrous results. By now, fans were yelling from the stands for the coach to run another play. But the coach wasn't swayed. After three more failed attempts, he yelled, "Punt!"

Giving in to the coach's stubbornness, the players

huddled on their third offensive possession, resolving to quit complaining and just run 37x the best they could. On first down the quarterback handed off to the fullback and *boom*—a three-yard gain. Wow! On second down, 37x went for five more yards. On third down and two, the fullback, behind the blocking of the linemen, went for thirty yards. Confidence and excitement grew. On first and goal from the eight-yard line, the wide-out came from the sideline with the next play. The quarterback, dismissing the receiver before he ever spoke, said, "We know: Thirty-seven X."

"No, no!," the receiver replied. "Coach said run any play you want."

Amazed, the quarterback turned to the linemen and said, "What play do you want to run?" The reply came in unison: Thirty-seven X." The result, *touchdown*!

The rest of the game was easy. The fear was gone.

The team's confidence and belief in themselves was established. The final score was a blowout but, more important, the team had learned their lesson. As the coach would say, If you keep running away from what you fear, you will run out of places to hide.

"Don't run away from your fears, run right at them!" It was a lesson for a lifetime, taught through a simple play—37x. ■

$\mathscr{L}$IFE IS A $\mathscr{W}$ORK IN $\mathscr{P}$ROGRESS

Life is a work in progress
that never is complete.
We learn a different lesson
from each experience we meet.

We learn the joy of living—
of what a heart is for.
We learn that through our trials
we are stronger than before.

We learn the thrill of victory,
the pain of a defeat.
We learn, to win the battle,
we must first learn to compete.

We learn from our reactions
to things we can't control:
There are times we should hang in there
and times we should let go.

And if we keep on learning,
if truth we try to find,
the wisdom of the ages teaches—
Keep an open mind.

These lessons that we gather
as we travel on our way
help complete the work in progress—
a fulfilled life someday.

LET THEM PLAY

WITHOUT A DOUBT they were the craziest group of girls I have ever been around. They were also without a doubt the most fun. Angela, Angie, Kari, and Kara, along with their teammates, still occupy a special place in my heart. It's strange but this group of girls, who probably needed discipline more than any other team I ever coached, taught me a lesson on letting go of control, having fun, and trust.

I believe in discipline. I believe in team play. To that end I felt it was my job to teach those beliefs to this eighth-grade basketball team. It was not going to be an easy job. Loaded with talent, this team of girls was also loaded with a bunch of free spirits. They were constantly doing things that would make me want to pull my hair and laugh at the same time. I *will* say this about them— they cared for each other and they all wanted to win.

Halfway through the season we faced our toughest challenge, a team that was undefeated, as we were, and with a lot more talent. The game began and we battled to a small halftime lead. I coached the first half in my usual demanding manner, trying to control every move my players made in order to ensure victory. The second half was playing out the same until late in the fourth quarter. With five minutes to go in the game the referee blew his whistle for a time-out. During the time-out the officials conferred with the scorers table and decided to make a correction in the score. Our six-point lead suddenly shrank to a slim two-point margin. I was livid. I protested the decision loudly, but I couldn't risk a technical foul that would give our opponents two free throws plus the ball. Frustrated, I put a towel over my head and sat down on our bench to pout. The girls gathered around me for instructions, but I was too upset to speak. Finally, Angela, our point guard, spoke up, "Don't worry, Coach, we'll beat 'em."

Sitting on the bench with the towel over my head, I watched as the girls walked back to the court. Still sitting there, I saw them huddle together on their own to plan their strategy. When play resumed, I watched as they ran a stall to protect the lead. Eventually, the other team was forced to foul and I watched as time and time again the girls made free throws to increase our lead.

That is when I noticed a change. Instead of trying to control them, I found myself cheering for them. The game ended with a victory. I was so proud of those girls! They had taught me a valuable lesson.

The rest of the season I looked at that team differently. We still had discipline. We still emphasized teamwork. But we also emphasized having fun. I learned to trust them and enjoy them as a great group of people, not just players. Keeping that in mind, I just "let them play" the rest of the year, and winning took care of itself. ■

*T*EAM

What does it mean to be part of a team,
working with others, sharing a dream?

What can you gain by playing this way,
as part of a group, not only your way?

You learn how to give and how to fit in,
that helping each other is the best way to win.

You learn how to trust and to be counted on.
No matter the outcome, you aren't alone.

You learn to encourage when confidence lacks
and how to accept a friend's pat on the back.

And when things get tough, when troubles begin,
you all hang together through thick and through thin.

What do you learn when you play as a team?
You learn about life and what true friendship means.

3

*G*IVING
OF
OURSELVES

LIFE TEACHES US
THAT WHAT WE WANT
IS NOT NEARLY AS IMPORTANT
AS WHAT WE GIVE.

$\mathscr{W}$HAT IS $\mathscr{G}$REATNESS?

FRED HARRIS SET A single-season scoring record for our high school basketball team his junior year. What happened Fred's senior year taught me that he was more than just a great player.

When we lost the first game of the season that year, it became clear that the same scenario would be repeated consistently all season. Fred was the only player with varsity experience. The rest of the team had graduated. During the games Fred would score his twenty-plus points, but it was never enough to pull the team to victory. The younger players were trying their best, but they needed time to learn and develop. Five games into the season we were still winless.

One night after a close loss to our nearby rival in an away game, I boarded the bus to find Fred staring out the window. His eyes were reddened and his face saddened by the sting of defeat. When we arrived back at the school I called him into my office.

"What's wrong?" I asked, although I already knew the answer.

"We're not going to win many games this year, are we, Coach?" Fred asked solemnly.

I couldn't lie to him. "Probably not."

Fred sat silently on top of my desk, knowing his senior year was not going to be the kind he had hoped for.

"Fred, you're not responsible for the situation you're in, but you *are* responsible for how you react to it. Your teammates are doing the best they can. Try to stay positive."

Fred left my office without saying a word.

I noticed a change in Fred after that. For the rest of the season he still seemed to be doing the best he could, but instead of getting upset over the losses, he took on the role of mentor for some of his younger teammates. That's the kind of person he was.

Near the end of the season, a college coach saw Fred play while scouting players on the other team. The next day I received a call from him. He asked me how Fred had handled the adversity of being such a good player on a struggling team. "He never criticized his teammates. He never criticized his school. He never criticized his coach," I said. "He became a true leader."

A few weeks later, Fred signed a scholarship to play basketball at the scout's college. Fred's dream, which had seemed so hopeless, had come true.

I once read that if you really want to be great you must give up what you want and learn to serve others. Fred Harris was more than just a great player. Fred Harris was a great human being. ■

*W*HEN LIFE HANDS
YOU THE BALL

What will you do—how will you act—
when hurdles stand so tall?
Will you rise up and do your best
When life hands you the ball?

Will you give up when filled with doubt,
Or will you give it your all?
The choice is yours—you get your chance
when life hands you the ball.

If you're prepared to face the test
When backed against the wall,
You'll hold the future in your hands
And seldom will you fall.

And never will the forces win
that make you feel so small.
At last—someday you'll find you dreams
when life hands you the ball.

HEART OF A CHAMPION

I FIRST MET DONALD JENRY when he came out for the eighth grade basketball team at our school. I was a young coach with still much to learn, and little did I realize that Donald would teach me a very important lesson about life.

Donald was a neat kid with a wonderful personality. What made Donald's decision to try out for the team unusual was that he was born with

cystic fibrosis, a terminal disease that causes fluid to col-
lect in the lungs. Because of Donald's condition he was
very limited in what he could do on a basketball court.
As a matter of fact, Donald could barely run from one
end of the court to the other without bending over and
coughing to clear his lungs. Sometimes his cough was so
severe his face would turn blue as he gasped for air.

When the time came to make cuts for the team,
I decided not to cut Donald in spite of his limitations.
During the games I would send him in once during each
half. Each time he would be able to run the court only
once or twice before he would have to come out
because of coughing.

The lesson Donald taught me happened one day
during practice. At the end of each session the players
would line up for conditioning drills. All the players
dreaded these drills because they were so physically

demanding. Donald always tried to keep up with his teammates, but the coughing would eventually cause him to drop out. The coughing was especially severe this day, so I went over and told him he didn't have to finish the drills if he didn't want to. Just the regular practice was hard for a person with his condition. "Oh, no, Coach!" Donald said, "I'm not going to quit. I'm going to keep on going. I'm going to make myself better. Better for myself, better for the team."

I knew I was witnessing something special. Despite his physical condition, Donald was determined to make himself and the team around him better. He could have sat out those conditioning drills, but he turned and joined his teammates as they continued their running.

Donald Jenry lost his battle with cystic fibrosis the following summer. He died with little fame and little fanfare. But he died with the admiration and the respect of all who knew him. His spirit to live, to continue to try, to continue to grow—to fight to win, despite the odds—taught me a lesson I will long remember. ■

*L*IFE'S NOT ONLY ABOUT ME

Though my troubles and my worries
are sometimes all that I can see,
still, I always must remember:
Life's not only about me.

Other souls are also hurting,
and I know that it is God's plan
to reach out to help another,
to extend to them my hand.

With this purpose as my focus—
to be a comfort to a friend—
all my troubles and my worries
seem to fade out in the end.

It is one of God's true lessons,
how life's walk is meant to be:
"True happiness I find when
life's not only about me."

4

$\mathcal{F}$OLLOWING YOUR DREAMS

SOMETIMES ALL A
DREAM NEEDS IS FOR
SOMEONE TO BELIEVE . . .
AND IT CAN COME TRUE.

NEVER GIVE UP ON YOURSELF

SOME PEOPLE THINK coaches should have all the answers. The truth is, nobody has all the answers. While coaches spend countless hours preparing their teams for victory, from time to time something totally unexpected happens. Those unexpected surprises can make special memories.

When Brandon was a freshman, he was so skinny he had barely enough strength to dribble a basketball, but that didn't stop him. Any time there was an open gym or a pickup game, he was always there. He just loved to play. If you had asked me what Brandon's chances were of ever playing varsity basketball, I would have told you they were not very good.

When tryouts for the freshman team were conducted, Brandon was the last one to get a uniform. He didn't play very much that year, but it didn't seem to bother him. He never missed a practice and seemed to enjoy just being part of the team. His sophomore year was much the same. Brandon was always there—every practice, every open gym—always around. He never complained. He never pouted. He always had a positive attitude.

Tryouts his junior year were another close call. He had grown a little, but he was still small for his age. As coaches, we agonized over whether to keep Brandon one more year or let him get on with his life outside of basketball. We thought about asking him to be a manager for the team. The decision came down to his attitude. Because he had been so loyal, we decided to give him one more chance. I remember watching Brandon shoot free throws during a junior varsity game that season, and the shots weren't even hitting the rim. I wondered if we had made the right decision.

The summer before his senior year, Brandon began to change. His body hit a growth spurt; his height shot up to six feet three inches. He also gained strength as he put on weight and kept it on. At a summer basketball camp, the coaches remarked to me how impressed they were with his game. If they only knew how far this young man had come!

His senior season began, and Brandon—who had almost been cut the three previous years—earned a starting role. He was both proud and determined not to let anyone down. He had a wonderful season that year. Brandon became one of our team leaders. For his play he was awarded Honorable Mention All-Conference by the other coaches in the league. Not bad for a skinny kid with little chance of ever making the team.

Brandon's story is an inspiration to all those who know the feeling of sitting on the bench waiting for a chance to play. He loved basketball, so he never gave up. He kept on trying. He is living proof that coaches don't always know everything. Surprises make better memories. ▪

GET INTO THE GAME

Standing on the sidelines
isn't quite the same.
To live a life worth living,
you've got to get into the game.

Looking toward the future,
trying to prepare,
waiting for your turn to play
doesn't seem quite fair.

But the will to be a winner
won't accept the words "I quit."
It makes you keep on trying
when others choose to sit.

And finally when you're ready,
when life gives you a chance,
you find the joy of living
when you step in the dance.

Standing on the sidelines
isn't quite the same.
To live a life worth living,
get into the game.

THE CARD STORY

I REMEMBER HOW I felt when the idea hit me. Thrilled and certain. Ready!

I was in algebra class; it was spring of my junior year in high school. The football season was long over, and the next was a long way off. We had done well that season—qualifying for the playoffs for the first time in school history— and I wanted us to do even better the next year, my senior year. But how? Suddenly, I knew. I didn't wait for after school. During my lunch break, I drove to a print shop and ordered business cards with a simple, direct prophesy, BOONVILLE PIRATES—1974 STATE CHAMPIONS!

When the cards were ready, my teammates and I distributed them all over town. Teachers pinned them to classroom bulletin boards. Merchants taped them to store windows. Pretty soon those cards were everywhere; there was no escaping them. That's what we wanted. We wanted our goal to be always in front of us, for everyone to see, impossible to overlook, no matter where we were.

By the time football practice started in late August, we were focused. A sense of direction and unity pulled us together as a team. From day one we gave more in practice, paid more attention to detail, executed assignments more sharply. With the goal imprinted in our minds and hearts—BOONVILLE PIRATES—1974 STATE CHAMPIONS!—we marched through the season undefeated and went into the playoffs with a sense of destiny.

The first playoff game matched us against a power-house team that was riding a 28-game winning streak. We knew we were in for a fight, but as the intensity of the game increased, so did our determination. We won, pulling away in the second half. That took us to the brink of our goal, a matchup with the defending state champions for the title.

We began preparing for the big game with the same calm intensity and focus we'd shown as a team all season. Then it started to snow. A huge storm blew in. School was canceled; roads were closed; transportation systems shut down. Still, every member of the team made it to the school gym, and we practiced for the biggest game of our lives in tennis shoes. We heard that the state officials were thinking of canceling the game and declaring both teams co-champions. We continued with practice anyway. No way, we thought. This was our year.

On Saturday, we arrived at the stadium to find a white playing field. The goal posts stuck up out of six to eight inches of snow. Undaunted, we dressed for the game and began our warm-ups.

Both teams struggled through to a scoreless first half. In the locker room at halftime, our coach reminded us of all we had been through to get to this moment. "Remember your goal. Remember your focus. Remember—*the card!*"

Playing conditions were as tough the second half as they were the first, but our determination wasn't numbed with our fingers and toes. We hung in there and pulled away in the second half, scoring 34 points to their 14.

Our year-long goal was fact: The Boonville Pirates *were* 1974 state champions.

And yes, I still have my card. ■

*O*DE TO THE CHAMPIONS

Who are these people,
these doers of deeds,
these dreamers of dreams
that make us believe?

Who are these people
who still win the day
when the odds are against them
and strength fades away?

These people are champions
for they never give in.
A heart beats within them
that's destined to win.

57

They follow their dreams
though the journey seems far.
From the top of a mountain
they reach for a star.

And when they have touched it,
when their journey is done,
they give us all hope
from the victories they've won.

So here's to the champions—
to all their great deeds.
They follow their hearts
and are winners indeed.

5

$\mathscr{M}$AKING A DIFFERENCE

EVERY PERSON NEEDS A FRIEND,
A CARING, NURTURING, ENCOURAGING
FRIEND. FRIENDS GIVE GUIDANCE.
FRIENDS GIVE HOPE. FRIENDS HELP
YOU ACCEPT YOURSELF FOR
WHO YOU ARE. FRIENDS ARE
THE WORK OF ANGELS.

*M*Y TEACHERS

I once met a teacher who taught me to read
and how to spell words that I someday would need.
How could she have known where
her lessons would lead—
when she shared her gift with me?

I once met a teacher who taught me to sing.
A song in your heart is a wonderful thing.
I wonder if she knew the joy that would bring—
when she shared her gift with me?

I once met a teacher who taught me to draw.
She opened my eyes to the beauty I saw.
She taught me to see there is grace in us all—
when she shared her gift with me.

I once met a teacher who taught me to play
as part of a team, not always my way.
He taught me a lesson on sharing that day—
when he shared his gift with me.

I once met a teacher who taught about life—
to believe and have faith during good times and strife.
I wonder if he knew his words would give light—
when he shared his gifts with me.

All of these teachers shared gifts that were free.
What I do with them now is all up to me.
If I share them with others how glad they will be—
that they shared their gifts with me.

My Dad

THE EARLIEST MEMORY I have of my father is of me, grabbing his hand, and of him, guiding me as we walked together. I'll always remember that.

When I was a little older, my dad and I would listen to the high school basketball games together on our transistor radio. I would write a list of the player's names on a piece of paper and keep track of each boy's points as the game played out. I was so young I always fell asleep before the game was over. The next morning I would wake up in my bed with the score sheet lying next to me, completed by my father before he carried me to bed. I'll always remember that.

My father was a bread man—he delivered bread to the grocery stores early each morning. Sometimes, my father would bring his truck by the house early in the morning on cold days when I was home from school over Christmas, and I would ride on the floor of that truck as he made his deliveries. The rich smell and the warmth of the fresh bread made my mouth water and kept me warm at the same time. I'll always remember that.

In high school I went out for sports, and my father attended all my games. Senior year, our football team qualified to play in the state championship game, for the first time in the school's history. The night before the game, my father came to me and explained sadly that he would not be able to be there—he had to deliver his bread first, and the game was a three-hour drive from his route—but he said he would listen to the game on the transistor radio. I said I understood.

The next day as game time approached, I thought about my dad. As we lined up for the opening kickoff, I happened to look across the field to the parking lot— and his bread truck was pulling in. He had made the game, and we won the state championship. I'll always remember that.

Years later, after I had become a teacher and a coach, my wife and I were awakened by the sound of the telephone at 5:30 A.M. I struggled to the kitchen to answer the phone. I'll never forget the sound of the sheriff's voice on the other end, telling me Dad had just been killed in an automobile accident on his way to work. Cattle from a nearby farm had broken through their fence and wandered onto the highway. It was a dark, rainy morning, and my father had not seen them as he came over the ridge. The impact spun his car sideways in the highway, where a semi collided with it. The sheriff said he died instantly. I was devastated. I could hear my heart beat in my ears. I hung up the phone and walked back into the bedroom and sat on the edge of the bed. My wife kept asking me who was on the phone, but I couldn't speak. The hardest thing I've ever done in my life was finally to say the words, "My dad is gone." I'll never forget that.

After that, things didn't really matter to me. I went about my life but I didn't really care. It was as if someone had taken my heart out of my body, and I was just a robot. I went to work, I still taught school, but I was just going through the motions.

One day, as I was supervising a first-grade recess,

something happened that I could not have foreseen. A
little boy walked up to me and grabbed my hand. His
hand held mine the same way I use to hold my father's
when I was his age—by the last two fingers. In that
instant my father came back to me. In that instant I
found my purpose again. You see, even though my father
was gone he had left something with me. He left me his
smile. He left me his compassion. He left me his touch.
I began to realize that my purpose was to use those gifts
as he had. And from that day I started forward. ■

$\mathscr{P}$LAY CATCH
WITH ME, DAD

"Play catch with me, Dad?"
I hope you don't forget
about the little kid at home
with the baseball and the mitt.

I know that you are busy
with important things all day,
but it makes me feel so special
when you take some time to play.

Learning how to throw and catch
won't mean that much to me.
It's just the being with you
that makes us family.

So even if you're feeling tired at night
from the day that you just had,
please don't forget I love you
and play catch with me, Dad.

THE BUMBLEBEE DRILL

AS SHE SAT IN MY health class the beginning of her sophomore year in high school, Crystal seemed to be just another anonymous face blending into the sea of new faces that I faced every semester. She seemed to have a caring quality about her that made people feel comfortable, but there was something missing or empty about the way she would sometimes stare out the window.

One Friday, I decided to break the monotony of the class by doing an activity I called the bumblebee drill. We arranged half the chairs in a circle in the middle of the room. Half the students sat in the chairs while the other half stood behind them. I told the class that the people sitting down were the flowers and the people standing up were the bees. "It is the job of the bees to nurture the flowers," I said. They were to do this by giving the person sitting in front of them a nice shoulder massage while I played soft music on the CD player I had brought from home. Every minute I would say "Switch," and the bees would have to go to another flower for nurturing. Then, the students would trade places, with the flowers becoming the bees and the bees the flowers.

Things were going fine until a student came up to me and said, "Coach, Crystal is crying!" I went to Crystal and found her weeping quietly as she sat in her chair.

"Crystal," I whispered, "what is wrong?" "Coach," she replied, "my mother passed away two days before my eighth birthday. The song that is playing was my mother's favorite. She used to sing it to me all the time. My mother was always the one who gave me hugs and made me feel special.

"Coach," she said, "I miss my mom."

By now the whole class had stopped and was looking at Crystal. They were concerned. I asked her if any of her classmates knew this story. No, she said, it was something she'd always kept to herself. I asked her if she would share her story with them, and she agreed.

When Crystal finished speaking, you could hear a pin drop. I told the class I was going to play the song again for Crystal and her mother. "Crystal may get a little sad," I said, "but that's okay because they are sad tears for happy memories."

I started the music and witnessed a remarkable thing. One by one, the students came to join Crystal at the front of the room. Some of them hugged her. Some of them put a hand on her shoulder. Some of them just came up and stood next to her. Soon the whole class stood around her. When the music stopped, Crystal stepped forward and said, "Thank you. I feel like I have a lot of friends."

Crystal was never again "just another anonymous face." She became a friend to a lot of people that day, including me. ■

*I*T ONLY TAKES A MOMENT

It only takes a moment
to reach out to be a friend,
but to the one who needs you
the memory never ends.

A simple act of kindness
to a person you don't know
may plant a seed of friendship
that for them will always grow.

We sometimes lose perspective
of the difference we can make
when we care more for our giving
and care less for what we take.

So remember that your actions
may help change a life someday.
Always think about the person
that you meet along the way.

For it only takes a moment
to reach out to be a friend,
but to the one who needs you
the memory never ends.

6

GROWING

GROWING MEANS
CHANGING.

GOOD FRIENDS AND
GREAT MEMORIES
LAST FOREVER.

BECOMING

You are on your way to becoming
the person that you were meant to be.
Have faith as you go on your journey,
though the end may be so hard to see.

If you feel you are losing direction
that your footsteps are losing their way,
let your heart be the guide that will lead you
to keep you from going astray.

Remember, God always is with you,
if ever you should need a friend
to help with the burdens you carry
and guide you to peace in the end.

GROWING UP, GROWING APART

"THINGS JUST AREN'T THE SAME." Lacey said. "I really don't see that many of my friends anymore, not like I used to. It seems everybody is going her own way." Lacey and her friends grew up as teammates. From the time they were little girls they had spent their summers playing AAU basketball together. When they were old enough, they began playing basketball for their junior high school. They were always together. They were also very successful. Lacey, Courtney, Terianne, and Hope were definitely the leaders but Ashlee, Michael, Kara, and Jackie added their talents as well. All together they were a tough team to beat.

But now things were different. Their playing days had flown by all to quickly. As they stood on the brink of their senior year in high school—their last one together— reality was starting to set in. Since freshman year, they had been drifting apart, one by one, going their own separate ways. No longer did they all play on the same summer team. Basketball was no longer their sole focus. Some of the girls became interested in other sports: volleyball, softball, golf. Some became interested in other areas of life: jobs, cars, boys. Whatever the reason, Lacey was right. Things had changed.

Volleyball camp started. Adding to the feeling of

change was the fact that their volleyball coach had left for another job. Having to adjust to a new coach was not something these seniors were looking forward to. To say the least, camp did not start smoothly. It was time for a talk.

Before lunch on the second day of camp we had a little meeting. We discussed the frustrations they were feeling, and I tried to assure them that they were going to be okay. This was their senior year, and in order to enjoy it they needed to adjust. Reaching out to accept a new coach would be a big adjustment. Learning to accept the changes in themselves and their friends would be an even bigger one. After our talk I think they felt better. We all went out to lunch together and had Chinese food. It was Lacey's idea.

Life is a series of roller-coaster rides, full of unexpected surprises: highs and lows, sudden changes of direction, unexpected turns and dips, and then—the ride is over. All you are left with are exciting memories. But life itself is not over! You always have the choice of getting on with your life and making more memories.

Graduating from high school is only the end of one ride. In many cases it went by too fast. But in the end you are left with some wonderful memories of some wonderful friends. Your life after high school is the beginning of a new ride. You will never forget past memories, you will just make new ones.

Lacey is a pretty sharp girl. Maybe what she was feeling was a sad sense of growing apart. It's also an exciting part of growing up. ■

JUST ME

From the time I was little I knew I was great
'cause the people would tell me,
"You'll make it—just wait."
But they never did tell me how great I would be
if I ever played someone who was greater than me.

When I'm in my backyard, I'm king with the ball.
To swish all those baskets is no sweat at all.
But all of a sudden there's a man in my face
who doesn't seem to realize I'm king of this place.

So the pressure gets to me, I rush with the ball.
My passes to teammates could fly through the wall.
My jumpers not falling, my dribbles not sure.
My hand is not steady, my eye is not pure.

The fault is my teammates—they don't understand.
The fault is my coach's, his terrible plan.
The fault is the call by that blind referee,
but the fault is not mine—I'm the greatest, you see.

Then finally it hits me when I start to see
that the face in the mirror looks exactly like me.
It wasn't my team who was dropping the ball,
and it wasn't my coach shooting bricks at the wall.

That face in the mirror that is always so great
has some room for improvement, instead of just hate.
So I stopped blaming others and started to grow.
My play got much better, it started to show.

And all of my team didn't seem quite so bad.
I learned to depend on the good friends I had.
Now I like myself better since I started to see
I was lousy as great—I'm much better as me.

$\mathcal{W}$HAT IS IT LIKE TO BE SHY?

WHAT IS IT LIKE TO BE SHY? I posed this question to my high school health class when we were discussing a lesson on self-esteem. To explore the question further, I asked who was the shyest person in class. It was unanimous. Every student turned and pointed to Gary. There he sat, trying to disappear, with the attention of the whole class focused on him. He looked frightened. His classmates were right. This was one very shy sixteen-year-old.

I asked Gary to come to the front of the room and sit in a chair next to me. Reluctantly he accepted and came forward to take his place. I asked him what it felt like to be shy, but he never really responded. I then asked if he would take part in a little exercise that might help him with his shyness. He nodded, which I took to mean yes.

I scanned the room for another volunteer. It was easy to know whom to ask. Paige was a beautiful, bright, outgoing girl. A senior, she was older than most of the other students in class. She agreed to help and came to the front of the room, where she sat in a chair facing Gary. I explained to Gary that all I wanted him to do was to look directly into Paige's eyes for one minute. He didn't have to say it, but I could tell he was nervous.

"All you have to do," I said again, "is look into her eyes. Ready—begin." As the seconds ticked by on my watch, I watched Gary's face. It was incredible: I saw fear, sadness, loneliness, and pain. After the minute was up, I asked Gary how he felt. "Uncomfortable." was his reply.

I told him we were going to try it one more time, but this time I asked Paige to hold Gary's hands while the exercise took place. She took his hands in hers, and as Gary stared into her eyes this time, his expression was totally different. His face appeared more relaxed and at ease. There was also a look of peace in his eyes.

When the minute had elapsed, I again asked Gary how he felt. "Much better," he said.

What was the difference? I asked. "She touched me," he whispered.

Loneliness is not all it's cracked up to be. Have you ever felt different, as if you don't fit in? For most of us it doesn't feel very good. How many people walk the halls of our schools and no one ever talks to them? Gary felt more acceptance—more worth—when Paige touched him. Even though it was scary, it made him feel better. We can do that for other people, even if it is just saying "Hi" in the hallway. That acknowledgment may be just enough to make someone feel special and have their whole day be brighter.

What is it like to feel shy? It only takes a minute and a caring heart to say hello. ■

The Person That Is Me

If ever you should meet me
the image you may see
is just a mere reflection
of the person that is me.

The person I am really,
the one deep down inside,
is made of many feelings
that I sometimes try to hide.

Feelings of doubt and worry,
wondering how I will fit in.
Feelings of hope and longing,
that someday I might win.

Feelings of frustration
for answers I don't know.
Feelings for my loved ones,
relationships that grow.

Feelings of loss and loneliness,
of memories left behind.
Feelings of excitement
for what I have yet to find.

So remember when you meet me
the image you may see
is just a mere reflection
of the person that is me.

7

PEOPLE COUNT, PEOPLE MATTER

WE ALWAYS BECOME
THE PEOPLE WE LOVE.

CARETAKER'S JOB

Why do I see faces in faraway places
of people so hungry and cold?
What have we been saying with words
we've been praying—
why isn't our action as bold?

How long must we wonder of God way up yonder
and never reach out to a soul?
Well, maybe it's time we got straight in our minds
our caretaker's job here below.

To make life worth living use talent you're given
no matter how great or how small,
and soon we'll discover we've touched one another
the way that our Lord touched us all.

THE IMPORTANCE OF HOME

AS HE SAT IN MY HEALTH CLASS his sophomore year, the most noticeable thing about Jerry was his inability to sit still. He was constantly fidgeting and bothering the students around him. In the hall between classes he was always on the edge of a fight because of his quick temper. Whenever we had class discussions about current topics that affect teenagers' lives, Jerry always contributed and would usually come up with some very insightful comments. When it came to doing homework, however, forget it—he never turned anything in.

One day after class as I was straightening up the room, Jerry stayed around to visit. Trying to come up with some conversation, I ask him how his grades were in the rest of his classes. "Oh, Coach," he replied, "I haven't passed a class since I started high school."

"Really?" I said. "You seem like a pretty bright kid to me. What's the problem?"

"When I was in eighth grade," Jerry said, "I was an A student. I lived with my grandfather and my grandmother. My grandpa would take me fishing or to ball games. My grandma would cook and listen to my stories. I really loved them. But the summer after eighth grade, my grandpa died. Grandma was too old to raise a teenager alone, so I was sent to live with my parents.

"My parents have been divorced for a long time and live in different cities. At first I went to live with my mom but after a while she sent me to live with my dad. Coach, my parents really didn't want me. They were never home. They kept bouncing me back and forth between them. In the past two years I moved twelve times. Now I have a hard time concentrating, and I really don't care." With that comment, Jerry walked out the door of my classroom.

Jerry dropped out of school at the end of that semester. Again, he had failed every class and he finally gave up hope. It's a shame. I can't help wondering what Jerry's life would have been like had he not lost his grandfather. In every classroom Jerry walked into after that he was labeled a "bad kid." Maybe he wasn't such a bad kid. Maybe he just needed a home. ■

Memories of Home

Warm friendly faces
and hideaway places
and reading a book all alone.

Dreams of playing all day
with a friend far away
take me back in my mind to my home.

Memories from the past
help those special times last
as I walk in my present each day.

It's a comfort to know
that wherever I go,
home is only a memory away.

In my children I see
reflections of me
as we spend precious moments alone.

It's for them that I pray
for special memories someday
of the place they will always call home.

■
■
■

$\mathcal{M}$OST VALUABLE $\mathcal{P}$ERSON

IN ATHLETICS WE SOMETIMES give an award to the MVP. This stands for Most Valuable Player. It is a way to recognize one person who has contributed the most for the good of the team. I thought it would make an interesting assignment to ask my class of teenagers who the Most Valuable Person in their life would be. What happened touched the heart of everyone in the room.

When April walked to the front of the class

that morning, none of us were prepared for what she was about to say. She was a quiet fifteen-year-old whom most students only knew as a girl who missed a lot of school. As she began to speak, the quiver in her voice betrayed her nervousness. She spoke quietly.

"My Most Valuable Person is someone I no longer have. My Most Valuable Person was my mother." With that her head dropped and the room was silent.

To ease the situation, I asked April what had happened to her mother.

"My mother suffered from manic depression," she said. "She tried to kill herself three times. All three times I stopped her. The fourth time I fell asleep. When I woke up, I found her." Again, stunned silence filled the room.

"How old were you, April, when all this was happening in your life?" I asked.

"Ten years old" was her response. April went on to explain how after her mother's death she had trouble attending school. Could you blame her? She explained that now she was trying to do better and get her grades caught up because she realized the importance of moving on with her life and getting an education. It was apparent that she missed her mother deeply; her loss echoed through her words. When she finished speaking, several girls in the class went to the front of the room to give April a hug, and after she sat down we observed a quiet moment for a while, until it seemed appropriate to call on the next speaker. Inside, I think we all cried a little.

The next day we brought April flowers in memory of her mother. I use a saying when I'm coaching: "Struggles make you stronger." It is my prayer that someday April will experience many wonderful blessings. I think she deserves them. Her determination and strength to overcome the adversity in her life is an inspiration. In my eyes she will always be a Most Valuable Person. ∎

CARRY ON

At times when you feel troubled,
when happiness is gone,
look to the heart within you
for the strength to carry on.

In the heart you will find virtues
such as faith and hope and love.
Gifts that have been sent you
from a power up above.

It is faith that keeps on searching
for the joy the soul hopes for.
It is love that heals the spirit,
making it stronger than before.

And should your heart be broken,
if your strength should fade away,
the power of these virtues
will still win out the day.

So remember when you're troubled,
when happiness is gone,
look to the heart within you
for the strength to carry on.

$\mathcal{F}$IRST LESSONS

THE WORLD SEEMS
BRIGHTER THROUGH
THE EYES OF A CHILD.

CHILDREN'S EYES

What kind of world is it, my friend,
that little children see?
I wonder, Do they see God first
because they just believe?

Do they see strength in caring eyes
who watch them as they play,
or maybe love through gentle hands
that guide them on their way?

Do you think they dream of future times
when they would be a king,
or just enjoy their present life
while with their friends they sing?

Do they see the acts of kindness
done for people who are poor?
Is the very best in everyone
what they are looking for?

And when the day is over,
as they close their eyes to sleep,
do they look forward to tomorrow
with its promises to keep?

If this is what the children see,
it should be no surprise:
the world would be a better place
if we all had children's eyes.

THE STORY OF THE SEED

ONCE UPON A TIME there was a seed that lay upon the ground. The outer shell of the seed was very hard and solid and protected the inside of the seed from anything on the outside. Time went by and the seed never changed. Never. After a while the seed felt useless and wondered what its purpose was.

One day a caring gardener noticed the seed

and planted it in the ground. Rains soon came, and as the water seeped down through the ground and over the seed its hard shell softened and cracked. The crack allowed the water and nutrients from the soil to enter the inside of the seed. Then a marvelous thing occurred—the seed began to grow. A sprout sprang from the inside of the seed and began to struggle to work its way to the surface of the ground. As the sprout journeyed to the surface it began to grow roots to bring in more water and nutrients for strength. When the sprout finally reached the surface and peeked its head above the ground, the light from the sun shone on the sprout causing it to grow faster than before. Finally the sprout turned into a beautiful blooming flower. The bright colors of the blooms brought happiness to many people who passed by. Now the seed knew its purpose and never felt useless again.

Open your mind. Grow where you are planted. Find your purpose. Be happy. ■

Touch of a Friend

An angel was sent down from heaven one day
to visit a child who had nothing to say.
Now this young child was poor,
great wealth she did lack,
but she always was happy in spite of the fact.
Until one day it happened:
her friend went away,
and it left her heartbroken,
with nothing to say.

Now the task of the angel was a great one indeed:
to give hope to a heart that was so much in need.
And though great wealth and power
were at the angel's command,
he sent a lost puppy
and the healing began.

The girl cheered the puppy as he chased down a stick,
and she started to giggle as her face he would lick.
Then without any warning the girl whose heart broke
found some reason for saying
these words that she spoke:

"I love you, little puppy, I hope you will stay!
We will always be friends and together we'll play."

Now the little girl was happy—
though she still remained poor—
for she had a new friend, someone to care for.

You see, riches and power are fine things indeed,
but for a broken heart that is not what you need.
The angel was wise, for he knew in the end
how to mend a broken heart
with the touch of a friend.

THE INDIAN MOUND

IN MY HOMETOWN of Boonville, Missouri, there is an old Indian burial mound that sits high on a river bluff overlooking the Missouri River. It is said that a great Indian chief was buried there so he could watch over his vast tribe after his death. Standing on top of that mound one can see the river bottoms below for miles.

As a boy I use to love to climb up to the

mound just to sit and take in the view. I almost felt like I could touch the clouds from that high place. It was easy to use your imagination up there. Afternoons were spent just dreaming dreams of great things for the future. From that high place all you could see was the "big picture" as you gazed down below. Somehow my cares and worries just didn't seem as big while I sat there. I always felt closer to God on that mound.

I recently revisited that old Indian mound. It had been years since I had been there, yet the feelings were still the same. It was nice to escape once more to that place of solace—to sit on top of that hill and just enjoy the view. I needed to see the world from that perspective again and forget about my cares and worries for a while. Before long I found myself feeling better. I even started dreaming dreams of great things for the future again—just like I use to do as a boy. When it was time to leave I found myself recharged and refocused. Leaving brought on a sense of sadness—like leaving home.

I'll visit that old Indian mound again someday. I know it will always be there for me whenever I need it—just like an old friend. ■

$\mathscr{T}$HE LITTLE
BOY'S SMILE

There once was a village, a very small town,
where all of the people walked 'round with a frown.
They never were happy, they never were gay,
they just liked to frown so they did it all day.

One day a young boy from a faraway place
came to visit the people with the frown on their face.
This young boy was different, he did not fit in,
for instead of a frown he wore a big grin!

"What is he doing?" said the people in town.
"Doesn't he know that we all like to frown?"
"He doesn't belong." "He doesn't fit in."
"He looks so strange with that great big bright grin."

But the boy kept on smiling as he went on his way
until something real special just happened one day.
As he walked past the mayor,
whose first name was Jack,
He flashed his bright smile and the mayor smiled back!

"This feels so much better,"
said the mayor to the town,
"and the more that I smile, I forget how to frown."

So the people tried smiling as they went on their way
and they liked it so much that they did it all day.
And just like the mayor the townspeople found
the more that they smiled,
they forgot how to frown.

Now they all thanked the boy
with the smile on his face
for daring to be different from the rest of the place
and for sharing his gift—that he spread all around—
the gift of a smile that changed the whole town.

The Heart
of the Soul

As metal is forged by the fire
so to is the heart of the soul
made stronger by all of your trials
as you strive to accomplish your goals.

Nothing is real until tested;
you never know what you can do
until when the odds are against you
and you find the strength to pull through.

It's so easy to smile when you're winning—
when fortune is going your way—
but character comes from the struggles
of fighting life's battles each day.

So never back down from the fire
while striving to reach for your goal.
The trials you face on your journey
will strengthen the heart of your soul.

About the Author

Tom Krause has been teaching and coaching in the Missouri public school system for over twenty years. He is the founder of Positive People Presentations, a speaker's bureau dedicated to bringing out the best in people for their future. He has been published in numerous Chicken Soup for the Soul books as a contributing author. Tom's heartwarming presentations have helped thousands of people improve their outlook on life as well as their motivation as they face their world. Many schools and business organizations have found his popular presentations to be uplifting and beneficial. Tom is available for school assemblies, staff professional development workshops, and keynote presentations.

Touching Hearts, Teaching Greatness is his first book.